WAVE BOOKS SEATTLE/NEW YORK

IGGY

MICHAEL EARL CRAIG

HORSE

Published by Wave Books

www.wavepoetry.com

Copyright © 2023 by Michael Earl Craig

Wave Books titles are distributed to the trade by
Consortium Book Sales and Distribution

Phone: 800-283-3572 / SAN 631-760X

Library of Congress Cataloging-in-Publication Data

Names: Craig, Michael Earl, author.

Title: Iggy horse / Michael Earl Craig.

Description: First edition. | Seattle : Wave Books, [2023]

Identifiers: LCCN 2022045169

ISBN 9781950268795 (hardcover)

ISBN 9781950268757 (paperback)

Subjects: LCGFT: Poetry.

Classification: LCC PS3603.R3553 I38 2023

DDC 811/.6—dc23/eng/20221122

LC record available at https://lccn.loc.gov/2022045169

Designed by Crisis

Printed in the United States of America

9 8 7 6 5 4 3 2 1

First Edition

Wave Books 106

1

2

3

I'll feel terrible if you do it wrong.
And if you do it right, I'll feel even worse.

PEDRO ALMODÓVAR
Pain and Glory

1

THE TRAIN

I have a cheese sandwich in my briefcase.
No one here understands me.
The conductor makes his rounds,
wants my foot out of the aisle.
Taps foot twice with clipboard.
Then smacks foot pretty hard.

I need ice for my apple juice.
They found a gas leak in the snack car.
Cold blue rails take me toward you
as unattended pugs roam
car to car looking for something.

Daybreak; I head for the dining car.
They seat me with a stranger.
He tells me he's seven—says
he's an orphan. I order French toast
with sausage links and a side of bacon.
He orders the fruit cup with herbal tea.
At which point his parents arrive,

have been looking for him for an hour.
His mother is stone-faced. The father
begins to cry. The boy scoots over
and pats the bench seat beside him.

I lie in the dark on my side
thinking about the different
sides that I'm aware of.
The side of a horse.
The side of a ship.
(Old Ironsides.)
A side of beef.
A side of slaw.
Big spoon of mac & cheese
and its subsequent ramekin.
Then ramekin production . . .
the glazing of ramekins . . .
the inspections and the bubble wrap.

I extend one foot out
from under the covers.
The cover of night.
The album's cover.
The barbecue's, its
rustic joie de vivre in
waxed cotton duck.

If it looks like a duck, walks
and quacks like one it
might be a goose.
The goose who crossed the road.
(Why did she do it?)
And later the goose confit.
Meat in its own fat.
A fat lip. A fat knee.
The fatness of cats who
(I retract my foot)
can't fit through the door.
Not just a cat door but any door.
Any door that groans a bit.
Any door that vibrates.
The old door of redemption.
The door of deep feeling.

The grumpy castle owl last night
was communicating with other owls,
past owls. They spoke back
to him it seemed, from desolate trees
in the wetness of the rain.

They compared notes, owl notes,
remembering. They took new notes,
new owl notes, their future memories.

There was the baby one autumn—
they couldn't agree as to which autumn—
tossed from the bell tower.
It landed safely on a pile of twigs
the gardener had forgotten.

This baby went on to grow quite large.
Had dark sideburns resembling helmet straps.
Looked like a murderer his whole life
but was actually as meek as they came.
Had a beautiful singing voice.

Across castle grounds rolled a mixture of fogs.
Fogs from different centuries.

The owls called to this man. And waited.

A blind cat explored the dark basement
sniffing carpet swatches. Auburn nights
required auburn thoughts. The whole
family slept throughout the large house
in each of the many upstairs rooms
with each of their heads hanging
awkwardly over different edges of
their beds. Most aimed at the ceiling.
One aimed at an open window.
And one in one of the colder rooms
was aimed at an opened book that sat
on a dresser in another room.
Someone else's room.

Snow in yard looks fake
coming down, or maybe
digital, above reality,
staged somehow and moving
slower than snow should.
Big red chairs getting
snowed on, snowed past.
Cinematic. Wet books
on porch getting wetter.
Shit.

You say you like to think
your old bike might talk
to the canoe in the garage
when we're not there,
that even the dust has
thoughts, but it doesn't.
The garage is a vacuum.
You stir your drink with
your finger, a shellacked
look in your eyes.

I've shaved my beard
just as you start growing yours.
Why don't we hand-make
our own jigsaw puzzles you say,
before sitting down to work
on them? I reach over and stir
your drink with my finger,
a steady draft moving
from one cold end
of the house to the other.

Scrawny blind horses with stiff horse-dicks resembling ball bats
roam the plains from Vegas to Albany . . . big dicks banging on
old bathtubs and sagebrush. A few of you foresaw this.

A flattened glove on the barn floor, speckled with bird shit.
The transistor radio with dead batteries plays no George Jones.

PEP TALK TO SELF EATING
SALAD AT AIRPORT

Montana is the Italy of the New World.

Montana is God's Italy.

Montana is the Italy of the people.

It's the real Italy.

Italy *is* Montana.

Montana, the Italy of God.

Yes.

Like Italy only different.

Now that the corn is up and the hay is down.
Or that the hay is up and the corn is down.
Now that the scythes have been touched up,
have been oiled lightly and hung in the rafters.
Now that bucolic wonder has washed across the valley,
has flowed like champagne light into every nook.
Now that the wheat has been separated from the chaff,
never again one to intermingle with the other,
and the pheasant has been shot on the run,
or even if it wasn't running, and plucked
of every feather on the trail, in the dust,
and hung then from the pommel for any traveler to see.
Now that the horses have been greased
and carefully parked under waxed tarps
where they wait in beige box stalls for oats
and maybe apples. Now that night has fallen.
Now that the comet can be seen in the sky
but probably won't be, and the smell of baked bread
is moving through castle corridors, and the feeling
a foot might have, slowly pulled through a stocking,
is not entirely out of the question. Now that candles

are lit, that mice are on the move, that dried blood
has marked the stoop. It is now that I bend down
to lift the little one into position. Now that day's been
on the run and ran. And out from shadow steps my Stan.

JUSEPE DE RIBERA

Magdalena Ventura with Her Husband and Son, 1631

CANDLESNUFFER

Dogs on chains drag their small huts across the tundra.
Men in flannel pants are kneeling.
Opposite calmnesses interact.

IT WAS ABOUT TO RAIN

She looked maybe too much like
a young Claudia Cardinale.
She was agitated and banged repeatedly
her tiny espresso on its saucer
as aspiring monks on thin donkeys
entered quietly the square from different alleys.

An emperor tamarin worked the crowd
selling panatelas from a briefcase.
A diesel mechanic in a Berlusconi T-shirt
bought prosciutto and olives and sea salt.

It was about to rain and she waited
on pear spears with pine nuts, on a plop
of burrata with burnt winter rocket.
An older woman on a carbon-fiber fat bike
approached quickly the square, squinting,
feathering the brakes, her tires massaging
loose pavers. Strappy Roman gladiators passed
a pair of flat black shower sandals, Adidas,
and the panatelas were selling.
And then the rain came.

A wild-looking bonnet macaque chased
the cigar salesman beneath tables.
The wind picked up—an awning ripped
loudly, was torn from a building.
People ran, clutching their cheeses.
The gutters were gurgling. The macaque's bonnet
was bouncing. He couldn't stop burping.

PREPARING TO PAINT THE BODY OF
THE DEAD CHRIST IN THE TOMB

Did he think of himself that way,
as Hans Holbein the Younger,
standing yawning in the mirror?
He looked a little longer than usual,
then built up his bowl of pearled foam
and began to shave.

He'd ordered a corpse, it was on its way.
Fished from the Rhine
and he'd asked for a ripe one.

There was a horse, a horseman,
a long rope, a corpse
hauled onto the riverbank,
a running bowline tossed casually
around an ankle. The long rope
then tied to the saddle with
a gentle word or two for the horse,
a dirt-caked Friesian named Samuel
who misunderstood and began galloping.

As Hans shaved thoughtfully
beneath each nostril—

the horseman left standing
at the river—
this Samuel ran
as only a confused horse could
up the wet stone road,
into and through town,
dragging the tethered corpse
which leaked water and banged
disturbingly on the corners of buildings.
It went on for a while.

And because we believe
in poetry and uncanny timing,
it was precisely as Hans arrived
downstairs and stepped out
onto the front stoop
that this Samuel showed up
in a dash and braked—
a kind of sideways hockey-stop—
which brought the corpse
around nicely (albeit abruptly)
to the bare and bony feet of
the clean-shaven Holbein.

HANS HOLBEIN THE YOUNGER
The Body of the Dead Christ in the Tomb, 1521–22

CUBES OF ICE CLINKING

A medicine ball sits
all blau-schwarz
crushing carpet.
An accolade arrives
like a cut flower,
like old friends posing
as cadavers.

DOCTOR FAUCI

Through the garden he moves
like a flesh-and-blood C-3PO,
the last man standing
or one of three living people

okay seventeen but
of them he's one of
only three still gardening
and he does not have a mask on.

He goes up lane seven because
he calls all bean rows "lanes"
with a metal watering can
making little gestures with its spout,

tiny intuitive decisions for things
like beans and cucumbers,
up one lane down another
with no one to hump or to hug—

methodical turns of the wrist
of the wrist of the wrist—
shuffling casually toward sainthood
and compost.

CHOCOLATE SANTA

And one without names lay there bare and clean and issued laws.

RAINER MARIA RILKE

"Corpse-Washing"

supine

waxen

wide belt

stiff belt

gold plate

goodness

tin chutes

crucible

formidable

mandible

undressed

dressed again

cooling board

fingernail

foil

foil suit

foil being

the unbearable

lightness of

foil

red green gold

still

stillness

deadpan

the late lamented food

for worms

glint

wink

govern

It's late, can't sleep, the plane is loud, the plane is cold.
Your head makes me think of a watermelon,
or a block of wood or a wooden melon,
on a slender rubber stalk nodding,
nodding, snapping forward with force,
drool on your chin, drool on your shirt,
as pieces of trash move mysteriously
about on the floor between seats,
out into the aisle and back again—
a pamphlet on plantar warts,
a couple wads of cellophane,
some Kleenex, a soda straw followed
a minute later by another,
then a diaper, balled-up diaper,
and then the melancholy odor of balled-up diaper.

People are beginning to stir.
The food-and-beverage carts are moving about.
A pair of tortoiseshell eyeglasses
—folded, immaculate—
come gently vibrating down the aisle,

with sore passengers out for a stretch
stepping carefully over them.
These glasses take one look at me
and begin an awkward four-point turn
to head back up the aisle slowly.
To "only God knows where," I say,
when in fact it's seat 11D.

They appeared to be walking him, made his arms hang like cables.
A brass bell gently jingled for his one o'clock. He crossed
the shop floor nodding benevolently at the shop owner
and set one of the bags on top of a glass counter, which shattered
immediately—just blew to bits, left to right, like some kind of inside job.
Like a glass-counter conspiracy we'd all soon be reading about.
One of a number of shattering glass counters across this land and others.
Well-meaning salesmen setting bags down carefully.

Later, in the park, the salesman lit a cigarette. He loosened his tie.
His bags were on the ground near his bench, which made his shoulders
look different. The smell of cigarette smoke calmed him. A flood
of thoughts came randomly, images and emotions all at once,
and he opened a carton of noodles.

As the salesman rested, as he ate and smoked, the plants in the park
changed imperceptibly, were constantly morphing. A tulip underwent
sugar-density changes, was flexing, was turning to face different sunlight.
The salesman stabbed at his noodles and smoked and was happy—
a small piece of glass stuck to his sock—as a truck carrying Dixon melons
made its gasoline-leaking way across town, loose lids to manholes talking
back under tires, one-two beats, *cl-clanks* and *ch-chunks*. Like big coins
on the eyes of the dead, thought the salesman. He stopped chewing.

UNDERFOOT

The forest floor feels almost spongy with twigs
made from decomposing pianos.
Frogs relieve themselves on bark.
A toy dugout canoe carved by *the unknowns*
comes down the river.
We watch it. It takes forever.
Seems to be stalling.

2

Cowboy felt logy, looked and acted logy,
but according to his doctor was just aging.
Pirate wrote THE CRISIS IS NOW in mustard
on some lunch meat, then added cheese
and lettuce and a hoagie roll. Well over
one hundred candlewicks in the mansion—
it was Cowboy's job to trim them.
Pirate did rope tricks with his lariat which grew
increasingly stiff until it moved like taffy.
At thirty Cowboy added an eye patch
to distinguish himself from his colleagues.
Today he sat studying his hands, maybe
a couple calluses would suit him.
Calluses are mental said Pirate to Cowboy.
Cowboy thought about this.
Blood Pressures Plummet but Not Lifestyles
read the paper's morning headline.
Pirate reached over and circled it with his pencil.
So calluses are mental said Cowboy.
Calluses are mental said Pirate.

I won't cast aspersions said Cowboy.
Pirate did not believe him.
At noon the niece arrived, bringing
three tangerines in her mother's old fedora.

FIELD TRIP

I see tall grass. I see a lake. I see a dock.
I see a figure juggling lemons.
The choppy juggling of lemons.
I see parked mowers on mown grass.
I see a turtle who seems to both
resent and enjoy my dribbling
water on him from a bottle.
I see a wheelbarrow whose long
dry handles look almost Pentecostal.
I see a single mushroom, in the woods,
it is somehow frightening.
I see a trapdoor and go stand on it.
Nothing happens. Then comes
a tapering off, a tiring, a return
to the castle, if supper will have me.
As usual the castle turns out to be
a dense arrangement of shrubs
at the edge of the north end of town.
Three matches left in the matchbox.
It is beginning to snow.

AN ARM MOVING QUICKLY THROUGH
A COAT SLEEVE LINED WITH TAFFETA

The caddy hefted his divot absentmindedly.

In two out of three nightmares I
am grilling a flank steak.

A single lewd limerick changed the mood of the evening.

Lady Aberlin of the oarlocks.
Colonel Mustard in the cherry trees.
Lady Aberlin with a custard,
Lady Aberlin in waiting.
Colonel Mustard in the pantry with an almond.
Lady Aberlin in galoshes.
She is sockless.
Colonel Mustard often driving.
Toward Keeneland or away from.
Lady Aberlin, in waiting.
Colonel Mustard in a basement.
The treading Aberlin in water wings.
Colonel Mustard in the foyer.
Lady Aberlin in the foyer!
Mustard and Aberlin.
Aberlin and Mustard and Aberlin.
A circling and a dithering.
Wet lilacs. Vased umbrellas.

SPREZZATURA

To put your nose so far up another's ass
that your ears bend,
your eyes water,
your heels lift off the ground
a bit, as you press in there
so hard you do something
permanent to your cheekbones.
It's the nature of Nature.
It's a mysterious talking bow being lifted—
the bowstring being drawn
(two callused fingers)
and tall grasses, flattened by the wind.

PORTRAIT OF THE WRITER
MAX HERRMANN-NEISSE

He looks like a hunchbacked banker
crossed with a baby bird
who has fallen from the middle branches
(sound of nearby mowers)
his breathing untroubled
in the hand of a child
who with an index finger wants
of course only to pet him.
He stares off canvas at what?
I'm always wanting to know.
An unmarveling gaze.
One leg looks to have been swung
the way wooden legs often were,
up and over a real one.
Or even over a second one.
It's hard to tell because it's Berlin
in the '20s, all those wooden legs
coming in then from Rumburk
on the Spree, with good hinges
and shellac jobs that could stop
a luthier in the street. His head

is bald and large and veined,
appearing propped. He wears
a mood ring, pinky finger.
It's ruby red but can we trust it?
He will not budge, it's safe to say.
His lips are pursed.
His grip is gnarled—it's loose
yet tight. The streets are cold.
It's Tuesday night.

GEORGE GROSZ

The Writer Max Herrmann-Neisse, 1925

DRIVING HOME

Hundreds of finches in road
resting, drinking from puddles.
As I drive through them
they flutter up like sacred
soap-flake eunuch moths
and I think of the gaudiness
of poetry.

While reproduced often
no one bothers to
describe this.

Technique: Oil
Materials: Canvas/oil
Description: Description forthcoming.

And yet we know him.

Cloth a sailor's blue.
An allegorical blue.
The blue of the pallbearer?
A boutonniere blue.

Get closer.

The painting makes a sound—
air being released—
a light groan—
calf breath—
the squeak of leather.

Big leather chairs
and couches squeaking.
A settling into.
With lamps coming on.
It is dusk.

We know him.

FRANCIS PICABIA

L'Adoration du veau, 1941–42

CLOSING TIME

A farmer stands up in her field
crumbs of dirt dropping from coveralls
and begins to walk sideways
makes a sowing motion with right arm
her left hand in her pocket.

A pediatrician goes into a hardware store
and starts checking for swollen tonsils.

The farmer enters a dentist's office
in through the front door
heading straight to the back
loose bootlaces dragging
dirt on the carpet
dirt on linoleum
the Dremels softly whining
like distant snowmobiles
can she hear them?

The pediatrician drops to his knees
he is feeling for shin splints.

A few plumbers make bold gestures
wielding long pipes
while others use theirs to impersonate priests
making signs of the cross in the air
tapping people on foreheads.

The farmer enters Pillow Nation
in through the back door
makes her way to the front
past memory foam and goose down
past stacks of Japanese pillows
resembling pine boards
loose bootlaces dragging
speaking to no one.

It's five o'clock and dogs
lift legs carefully over everything
except hydrants.

The pediatrician raps an old man's knee
with a small rubber hammer
okay just relax for me he says
take a deep breath.

Toward them came the phlegmon.
You might expect it in a trash bag
but here it was in a bed on wheels.
It took two nurse's aides, one
at the stern and one at the bow.
Everyone moved aside as it passed.
People looked, couldn't help it.
"Keeps tracking funny," said one of the aides.
The bed kept bumping into things.
Seemed to move right at people.
And the phlegmon was tiny,
maybe 3 cm in diameter, was red
and wet and looked to be sleeping.
Swaddled in warm blankets.
It's what the nurses always fall back on.
Indeed the entire hospital staff.
Whenever something goes wrong
out come the warm blankets.

It's Christmas Eve, the church is packed.
Men in suits and ties, women in dresses,
children clothed as chips off the old blocks.

A beautiful child is carried in by her mother,
is then passed to her father who
bounces her a bit, turning to show her
her aunties who are laughing, lighting votives,
and then off she is handed to the priest
who's popped over for a visit.

The Christmas princess, dark hair pulled back
and tied with a bow, her dress a velvet bell
with white tights and patent leather shoes
that dangle gently during transport.

Then everything assembles. It is quiet. Mass begins.

The priest somberly fogs us, swinging
his thurible. I hear a baritone, and handbells.
People are kneeling; the princess totters

between them and the pew they lean on,
each person leaning back a bit to let her pass.

From where I kneel I can't really see her.
Only the slow-motion wave that she causes
along the backs of her relations.

It appears she is exiting stage left.
But when she gets there—someone in the choir
coughing—she turns around and starts back.

Moribund morning glories lifted lazily from the backcourt.
Two men set down bootwickers; the sinkhole shifted.
Tablezest is what kept us there, the flutehold is what brought us.
A wet marrowbone sailed through the air.

Without plantoscopy I was to be a different adherent.
Whitecaps full of marbles rolled in.
Crisped blueskins. A masterstroke.
The redundagym broke as banjos played the anthem.

Hammergogues and "red elves" stepped lightly over manholes.
For the showstopper poodles shook their heads at puddlecorks.
Blacksnakes drank white lightning from a thimble during *Star Wars*.
Then the baby shower. Then the nozzleburps.

RECOLLECTION

When I rolled the boulder from the opening it rocked back a bit
and got on my sandal. Not my foot but the tip of my sandal.
It took some effort to undo this.

THE RED MITTEN

A school bus is following me.
I stop walking, it stops.
I start again, it resumes.
The windows fogged.
This goes on for a while,
creeping across town.
I turn left, bus turns left.
I rub curb, bus rubs curb.
I stop again, it stops.
I take a step backward
and hear a gear grind.
A small red mitten wipes
the windshield. I jog
sideways like a sedated
horse dreaming and
bus doors open, let out
forty screaming children
swinging book bags.

The paperboy came every day at four,
only thirteen, drove dad's old DeLorean
with one gull wing open. He'd throw
the papers at the house—a slap against brick
or wood or glass, they'd make slightly
different sounds, depending.
Marsha could tell the difference
from any spot in the house—
folding laundry in the basement
she would cock her head.
She was a neighborhood legend,
had seemed ancient since the '80s,
got out and walked at least a little
every day, around the block, sometimes
twice. It's said she was a child in Berlin
at the Olympic Games in '36.
She saw Jesse Owens win gold
and the crowd go nuts as Hitler
remained seated. She punted a pit bull
once, I saw this, it was charging her.
Made it look like an accident, wearing

striped socks with sandals.
So it just wasn't like her to not come get the paper.
Neighbors saw the van and knew.
The men driving had matted hair.
When the sliding door opened
a styrofoam cup fell out. Some say
her legal name was Mona Catherine Lisa.
But everyone knew her as Marsha.

THE HONEYMOON

1

A coin dropped from the ship turned
flashing leaf-like through

an indifferent biome.
Metal trays brought ham

salad sandwiches down
the promenade deck.

2

Now was what she heard.
When in fact he'd said *Ow!*

3

A map unfolded itself

then refolded itself
on a deck chair.

4

The weather was changing.

When from a dream a sense of the festival emerged
I reached through and felt for the zipper,
for the tassel attached to the zipper.

A doll in a crate I'd just opened
looked up at me with a stoned gaze.

A series of damp cave chains
that only the dead knew of
ran through the base of a mountain.

Winter vegetables.
On a table in the courtyard.

Shapes of the hammer seen flashing
in the stream.

"Now is not a time for a toy"
said the repairman, who turned
the plastic dial. Broke it off.

Comes again that coppery time for naps,
domestic pyjama sharks swimming lazily
to the buoy and back. Rain barrels filling
as rain barrels will.

Sleepy blossom it was I and no one else
who jerked gently your chain at lunch, the bell
then hung in an oak to summon travelers.

3

THE HALF-PACKED SUITCASE

The half-packed suitcase unsealed a series of talking points,
of expungements verging on cannibalism. Was she coming
or going? It reminded me of modern nuns in quilted pantsuits
cracking open ball valves on bottles of sleep gas, the nurseries
instantly chilled, causing cradle-rock. It reminded me
that half the children in small towns across this country
were out stapling propaganda posters to power poles
while the other half sniffed airplane glue in basements,
their half-built biplanes waiting on paint-stained ping-pong
tables, on plaid ottomans and in the scuzzy bottoms of wall-
mounted utility sinks . . . it couldn't be helped. But in my mind
there was also a chance. As even a slug on a pearl hunt has
that wheel-of-cheese chance. That shirtless Duško-Popov-
doll-in-twill-pants kind of chance. And I turned in my mind
as one does in the sun. And reached up and shut the light out.

FIRST COW

It's a movie about a cow who shows up on a barge.
She belongs to one man but at night others milk her.
During the making of this movie no one wanted to squeeze
a real cow's udder, so they developed a mechanical cow
to use while filming. Then at night when shooting was over
all the actors and film crew ran into the woods
and milked real cows.

boats have been rocked—in good ways
but rocked

   and wrote

le barche sono state spaccate—in senso buono
ma sono state spaccate.

The only problem was the boats.
She said there was no equivalent
in her language.

Yes Italians have boats.
And yes a boat could be rocked.
But to *"rock the boat"* was something
untranslatable.

Besides, the way I had it was more
like boats were split, she said.
Split open on the rocks.
Which I rejected at first.
But later saw as nuanced.

He was galloping down the road toward Leeds,
his hat and jacket densely covered with black butterflies.
The recent rain had the marsh wrens trilling, shifting foot
to foot—the roadside ditches lined with knotgrass.
Wet cobblestones glinted, hooves clopped and slid,
smoked witch balls hung in nearly every cottage window,
and beneath all this his bib was stained—spilled port
and maybe pudding.

Something had called him and he was responding.
Like a wagon driver with a load of bone china.
Like Odo of Cluny scooching sideways toward Mary.
He closed his eyes (his horse didn't notice) and saw
seaside slot machines and a bowl of candlenuts
on a nightstand. A flute player's waxed fingernails
drummed unrhythmically. Who was she?
He jiggled the reins a bit.

He was near now and loped along a stone canal.
He saw a colony of ants float past on a loaf of rye.
He saw an ornate sign announcing The Worshipful Company

of Languor. A previously hidden canal boat now seemed
to be following him. The morning light hitting water
looked almost deep straw-yellow. A drunk man
threw perfect cleat hitches despite peeing his pants.
Also church bells, heard at intervals.
And noodle vendors down from noodle towers.
The very same noodle towers he had often dreamt of.

A baby had unswaddled himself, left blankets folded
on a park bench. A fountain gurgled, tossing ropes of water.
His horse walked now.
The man was shaking; someone threw him an unripe pear.
Then a sudden flash like a pain in the necklace.
He heard a rattle of loose pearls bouncing down
a steep staircase (or thought maybe he did)
as a hand reached in with a single horsehair for paintbrush
to add floating specks of dust to sunlight
streaming into dark bedrooms.

CHEMISTRY

They came from different worlds,
met at a masked ball, suffered
from different degrees of jet lag.
She was a sturdy woman, a religious woman,
she worked at the sawmill slabbing redwoods.
He was a fussy man, a tiny man,
a CPA with a deep love of birding.
She sometimes faked a limp, citing
the limp as a gateway to chastity.
He was a man prone to burying his head,
unburying his head,
burying his head,
unburying his head—
something he'd always associated
with irrational numbers.
She said her greatest pleasure in life
was to give a complete stranger a bath.
He had a mother he affectionately
called The Dock, who was constantly
almost completely surrounded by water.
He wore a suit made of feathers.

She wore clogs hewed from hardwoods
that knocked nicely on marble.
They took to the dance floor.
He touched her hand. She touched his cheek.

FINGER

She shook it, it shook back.
She saw this, she saw this.
She took it and tapped things—
the saucer, the Stilton.
She chased it, it poked her.
She swung from the oak beam.
She shook it, it shook back.
She swung from the oak beam.
A structural oak beam.

BOOTY

He shook it, it shook back.
He saw this, he saw this.
He took it and tapped things—
the Chaucer, the Milton.
He chased it, it followed.
He swung from the oak beam.

He shook it, it shook back.
He swung from the oak beam.
A structural oak beam.

ANKLE

She shook it, it shook back.
She saw this, she saw this.
He took it and tapped things—
the schnauzer, the schnauzer.
She chased it, it tripped her.
She swung from the oak beam.
He shook it, it shook back.
He swung from the oak beam.
A structural oak beam.

Due to the reaction-enhancing drugs I've been taking
the lower left side of my face sags during tennis.
It sags in the locker room and it sags on the pillow.
An owl pretending to be Joanne screeches over
and over again but with just the right pauses
for emphasis. I get up and crack the window a bit.
Recalcitrant chickens drawl chickenspeak into the millet hour.
I hear wine evaporating on the neighbor's kitchen counter.
Let's face it, I'm sensitive.

IGGY HORSE

a movement
glimpsed in a roar chorus

something seen between trunks

we shouldn't call the sunlight dappled—
the time for that is over

up the yellow hill
way up the hill toward the orchard

The father went to the window and watched.
It was one of three things he would do when this happened.
Large, dark clouds moved briskly over the land.
Made more dramatic by the occasional holes in them.

From his crib the son spoke to the father; inhaling
from a helium balloon had made his voice deeper.
He lay on his back and inquired about his mother.

I'M ASKING

1

A pale-blue trench coat sits up casually
on a big leather couch in the coffeehouse.

Casually but also inquisitively,
as often towels are draped,
as tarps are.

I look closer and see a pale waif
of a person inside, barely
there, totally naked, looking a little chummy.

Who does the talking here, God?

2

A Dixie cup blown in from Big Timber
comes skipping through the air
and hits me in the temple.

If the bushes are shaking, the wind might be blowing.

Sometimes a pony knocks over the cognac.
We flick chestnuts into the fire.

Who, God, is doing the talking?

BEACH SOUNDS

I'm like a piece of sea trash on the beach at night,
a tennis-ball can or part of a mannequin,
or someone's ring finger gently rolling in
like a small log turning over and over
—it pauses—before backtracking, small log
in reverse, the lullaby scour of sea-foam
calling back again this object, delicate wheel,
washed remarkably clean by salt water, by pebbles
and pieces of sea glass. I reach over and click
the clock light on—3:07 a.m.

I tug at the sheet which is tangled with the blanket.
A mannequin should never have to struggle with the sheets
is what I'm thinking, cranking myself around,
face down with right arm bent back awkwardly.
Adult Male, Realistic Face, Fiberglass Fashion Mannequin
with Base and Wig, #MR10–$268.52
Sounds reasonable. Add to cart? Let me think about it.
We're told do not stare gentle into that blue light.
Me lying here like a very clean tennis-ball can.
The sedative sounds of the ocean.
Like pink noise only better.

POEM ATTEMPTING TO DESCRIBE
AN EMOTIONAL CRISIS

Packed in sawdust sat the ice ax.
A cold réclame jostled.
I drew a parallelogram, you drew a parallelogram.

The senior book louse focused mainly on the Jameses.
A crayon came at me from the back of the nursery.
A single watt, walnut colored, bounced along the wire.

JEEPERS

Some horses won't drink if you're watching,
you have to drop the rope and walk away.
But Jeepers is not like that.
She is too well-adjusted.
She lifts her head and lets water
dribble from her mouth, a glimpse
of tongue poking out the corner
like a herniated bit of bubble gum.
And while nobody likes flies crawling
on them, Jeepers does not mind.
If she weren't quaffing like this
you'd think she were dead.
Only a dead horse allows a fly
to crawl all over them—Jeepers
has seven or eight on her face alone.
Is she okay? She isn't even blinking
and looks deeply up into the mountains,
water dribbling from her muzzle.
One fly in particular walks all over
her eyebrow, if you can call it an eyebrow.
Her heavy rope is soaked—also dribbling—
and her tail hangs limply like a curtain.

When they drained the town well
they found over forty thousand old tires,
hundreds of library books,
nine baby buggies and a manual typewriter.
There were no coins.

The tires were carefully removed
and tossed into the bay for safe storage.

An unmistakable voice
was coming from a tree.
We looked at each other.
We knew who it was.

"Does anyone happen to have a pair of tweezers I could borrow?
A dime has fallen into my piano."

We patted ourselves down,
each of us did,
for maybe two minutes thinking
wait, do I?

Then I patted you down,
checked all of your pockets,
and even where you had no pockets,
and you in turn patted me down front
and back, at times a little roughly,
saying things like "tweezers?" and
"any tweezers there?"

But none of this is crucial to the story.

When they drained the well
they found a rusted pistol
which was revealed to be a toy gun
at the exact moment that a second toy gun
turned out to be a loaded Glock.

Then they stumbled upon a very old set
of parallel bars in the woods
at the bottom of the well.
Which still felt remarkably solid.

WALLACE STEVENS HESITATING
BEFORE AN EVENING PLAYING BRIDGE

Like an applesauce company owner
who lies awake nights thinking
about that baby-food company accused
of having glass in its baby food,
he paused on the wet stoop before
ringing the bell.

It grew quieter and quieter the longer I walked. A blue heron
watched me, and feral cats darted into bushes looking cross-
eyed and scrawny. The road turned to dirt. Old men played cards
in groups. The younger men sat alone in lawn chairs, under
umbrellas, fishing for asp and common barbels, slingshotting
maggots over murky water. I kept walking.

There were the sky-blue eyes of a broken doll in matted grass.
There was a trampled turban, and what looked like a busted-off
stiletto stuck in mud. I continued along the road, it got narrower,
turned into a footpath. A rich mineral smell wafted in from
what might've been the center of all mineral industry. Which
was when I came across it, a canvas hug tent on the Tiber.

I pulled the flap back and stepped inside. And straightaway hugged
was I, by different people, of different ages and genders, some
hanging on longer than others, sometimes two at a time. An older
man hugged me hard, his face against mine—he looked through me
at the Big Nothing in the woods. And I let him.

NOTES/ACKNOWLEDGMENTS

Grateful acknowledgement is made to the editors and staff of the following
journals/anthologies where some of these poems originally appeared:
The Best American Poetry 2022, *Fonograf*, *Iterant*, *jubilat*, and *Sixth Finch*.

Many thanks to Chris Murray, James Shea, Susan Thomas,
and Matthew Zapruder for carefully reading and responding
to an earlier draft of this manuscript. Invaluable feedback.

Profonda gratitudine (and a round of chilled limoncellos)
goes out to everyone at the Civitella Ranieri Foundation.
This book would not exist without them. Grazie mille!

"Pep Talk to Self Eating Salad at Airport" is for Katie Balch. ;-)

"I Wanted to Say" is for Greta Caseti.

Rilke quote, page 24—translation by Edward Snow.

And finally I want to thank everyone, in all departments,
at Wave Books for their meticulous work, insights, patience,
and support. As always I feel lucky to know them.